A+ books

SIMPLY**SCIENCE**

KU-327-274

The Simple Science of
MAGNETS

Emily James

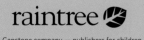

raintree

a Capstone company — publishers for children

Raintree is an imprint of Capstone Global Library Limited, a company incorporated in England and Wales having its registered office at 264 Banbury Road, Oxford, OX2 7DY – Registered company number: 6695582

www.raintree.co.uk
myorders@raintree.co.uk

Edited by Jaclyn Jaycox
Designed by Jenny Bergstrom
Original illustrations © Capstone Global Library Limited 2018
Picture research by Jo Miller
Production by Tori Abraham
Originated by Capstone Global Library Limited
Printed and bound in China

ISBN 978 1 4747 4350 1
21 20 19 18 17
10 9 8 7 6 5 4 3 2 1

British Library Cataloguing in Publication Data
A full catalogue record for this book is available from the British Library.

Acknowledgements
We would like to thank the following for permission to reproduce photographs: Getty Images: Visuals Unlimited, 20; iStockphoto: sturti, 26-27; Newscom: Digital Light/Richard Hutchings, 8, Universal Images Group/Dorling Kindersley, 14, 15; Science Source: Charles D. Winters, 9; Shutterstock: Algonga, 29 (sea turtle silhouette), Andrea Paggiaro, 21, AngelPet, 23 (inset), bikeriderlondon, 7 (inset), f-f-f-f, 11 (nail), Gerald Bernard, 24, Jan H Andersen, 10, Kawin Ounprasertsuk, 28, Malll Themd, 11 (paper clip), mangax, 12-13, Mega Pixel, 11 (magnet), Montri Thipsorn, 29 (inset), Olivier Le Moal, 4-5, optimarc, back cover (bottom), Peter Hermes Furian, 17 (inset), Pichet siritantiwat, 6-7, 28-29 (background), raduned, back cover (top), Sergey Nivens, 25, takasu, cover, Terrance Emerson, 18-19, Tyler Olson, 22-23, xtock, 16-17. Design elements: Shutterstock: bikeriderlondon

CONTENTS

Magic magnets

Magnets can make objects move – without touching them! When a string pulls something, you see it work.

But you can't see a magnet's power.
Magnets seem to move things by magic.

5

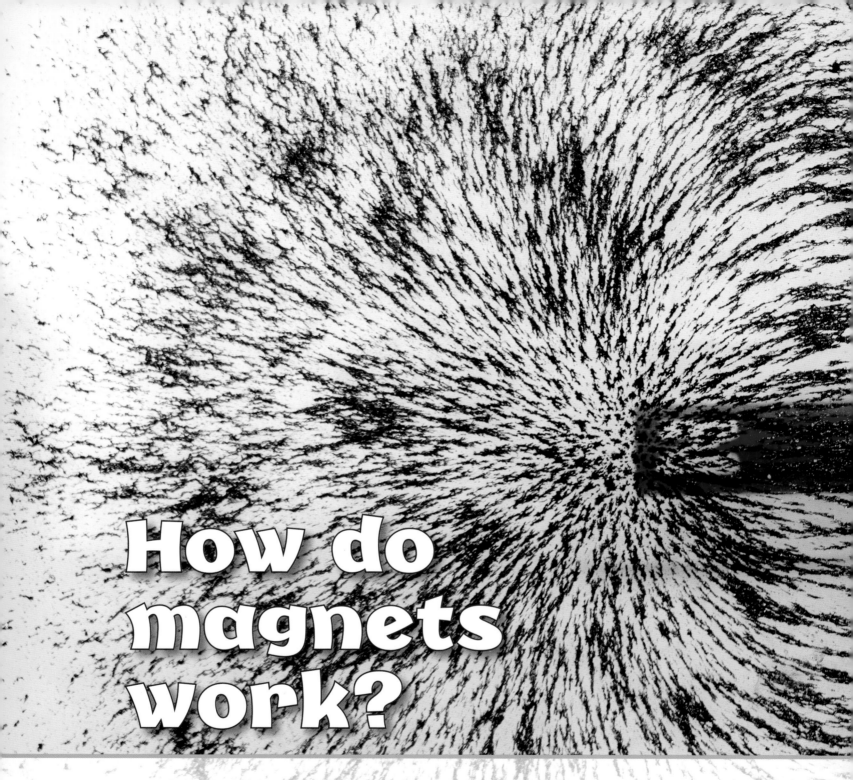

How do magnets work?

A magnet has an invisible area around it.
The area is called a magnetic field. A magnet
can pull things that are in this area only.
Place a paper clip far away from a magnet.

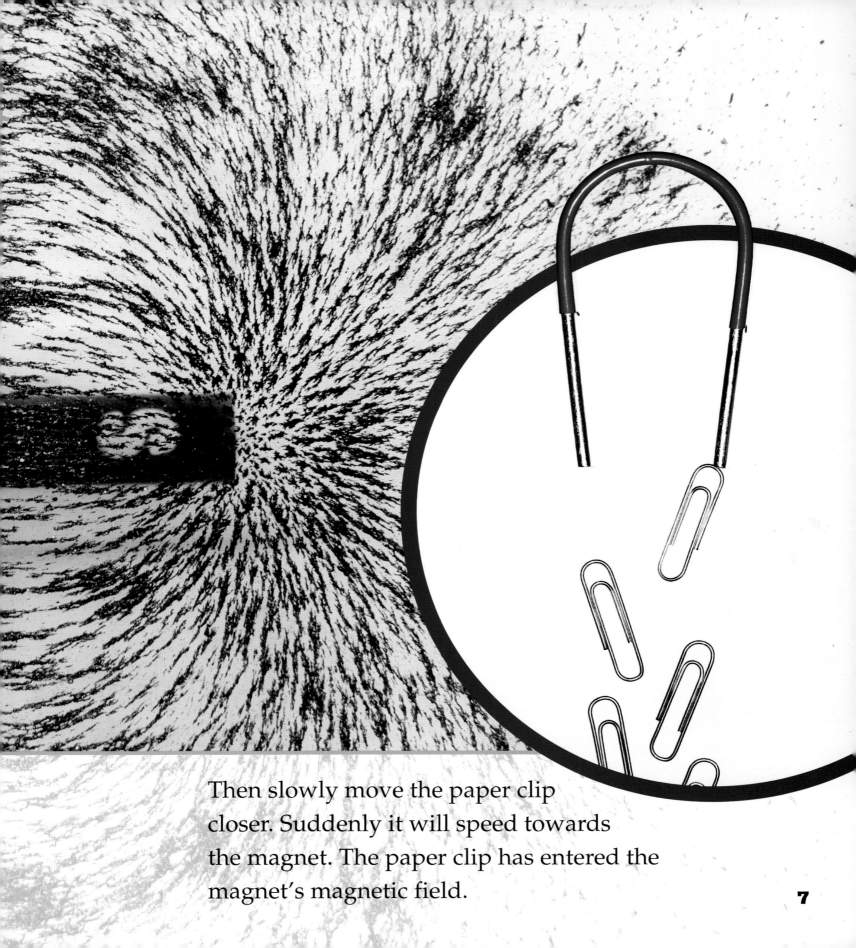

Then slowly move the paper clip
closer. Suddenly it will speed towards
the magnet. The paper clip has entered the
magnet's magnetic field.

Magnets can't move all objects. They move
only special kinds of metal.

Steel and iron can be moved easily by a magnet. Copper and nickel cannot. Neither can cotton, rubber or plastic.

steel

copper

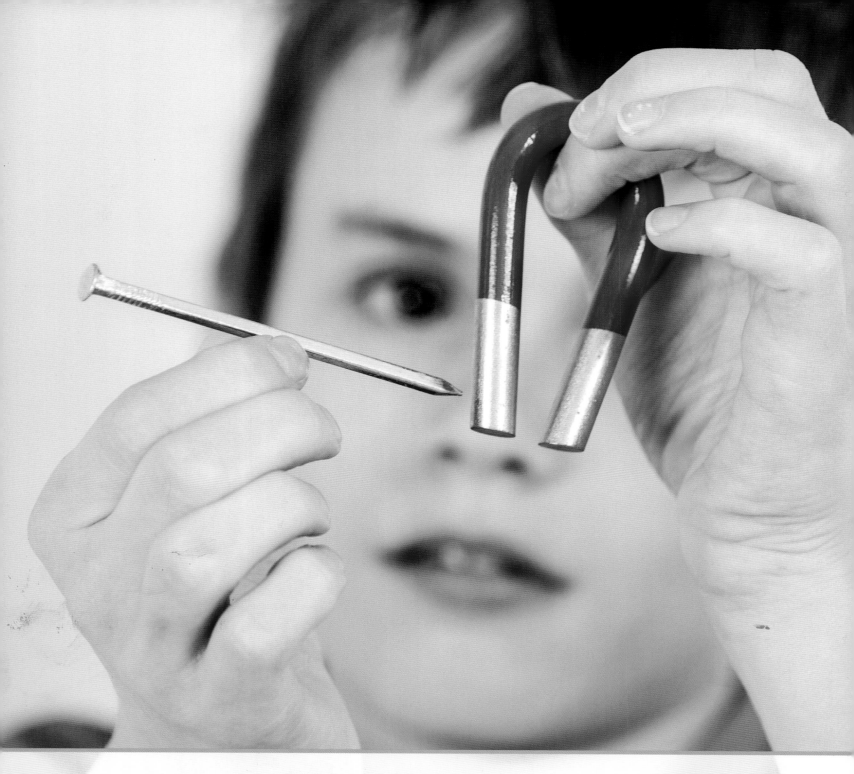

Magnets can turn some metal objects into
magnets. Try this: Hang an iron nail from the
end of a magnet. Then touch a paper clip to
the nail. What happens?

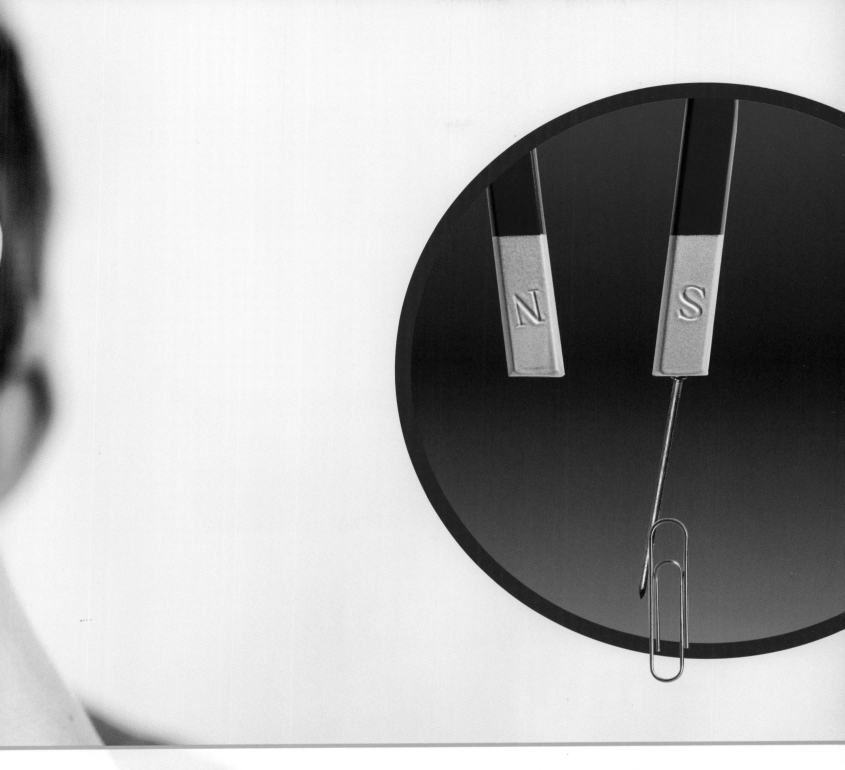

The paper clip sticks to the nail! The nail
has turned into a magnet. Now pull the nail
away from the magnet. Does the paper clip
still stick to the nail?

North and south poles

Most magnets look like bars or horseshoes.
Their power is strongest at the two ends.

One end is called the north pole. The other
end is the south pole. The poles can push
as well as pull.

Poles that are alike push against each other. They repel. The north pole of one magnet will repel the north pole of another.

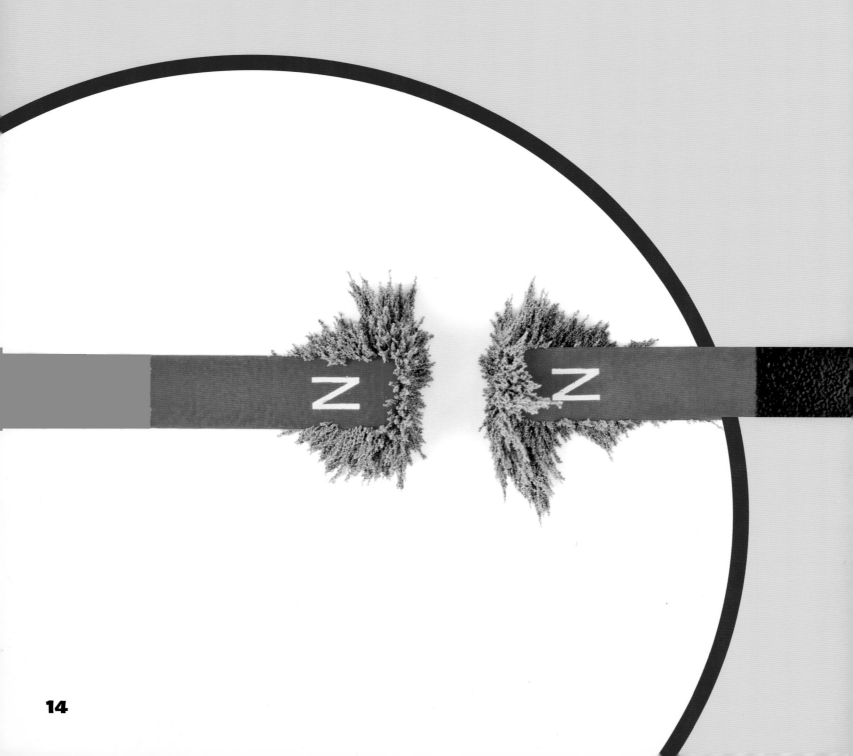

Opposite poles pull towards each other. They attract. The north pole of one magnet will attract the south pole of another.

Earth is a magnet

Earth is a magnet. A big one! Just like other magnets, it has two poles. Earth's magnetic poles are not in exactly the same spots as the North and South Poles. But they're close.

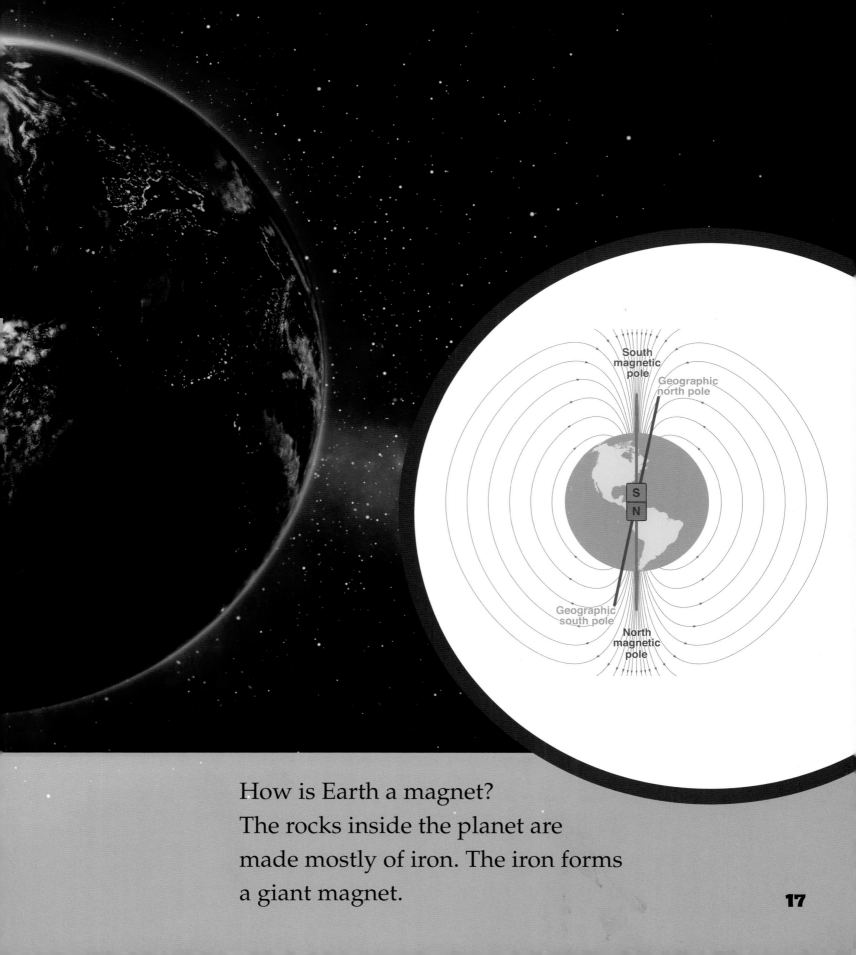

South magnetic pole

Geographic north pole

S

N

Geographic south pole

North magnetic pole

How is Earth a magnet?
The rocks inside the planet are
made mostly of iron. The iron forms
a giant magnet.

17

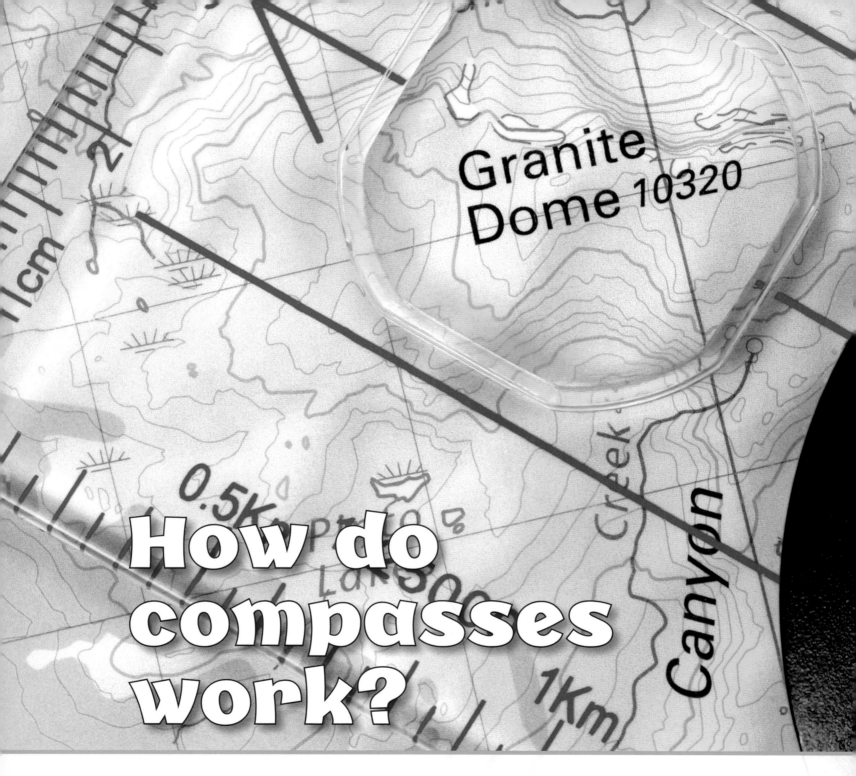

How do compasses work?

A compass holds a needle. The needle is a magnet. Earth's magnetic power pulls the needle towards the North Pole. A compass needle always points north.

Compasses help people find their
way. They show direction. Sailors use
compasses to cross the sea. Aeroplane
pilots and hikers use compasses too.

The first compasses were made from
magnetite. Magnetite is a black mineral.
It's a natural magnet. A piece of magnetite
is also called a lodestone.

Early Chinese compasses used lodestone.
They were carved into the shape of a spoon
and sat on a flat plate. The handle of the spoon
always pointed south.

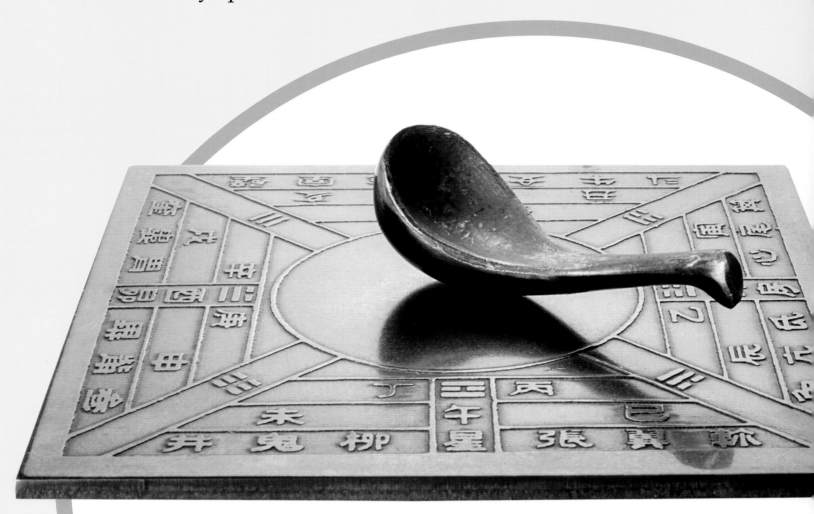

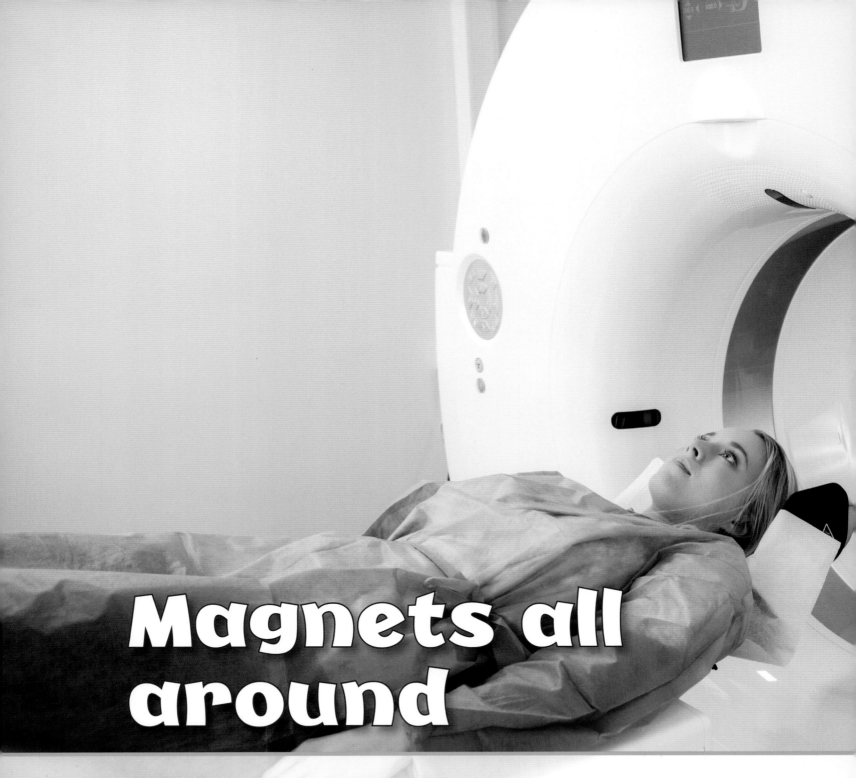

Magnets all around

Today we use magnets for many things.
Doctors use magnets to see where people are
hurt. An MRI machine holds a powerful magnet.
It helps make pictures of the inside of a body.

Magnets help scrapyard workers lift
tonnes of metal. The huge magnets move
cars as if they were toys!

Fans spin. Refrigerators hum. Burglar alarms ring.
None of these things can work without magnets.
Neither can TVs, radios or phones!

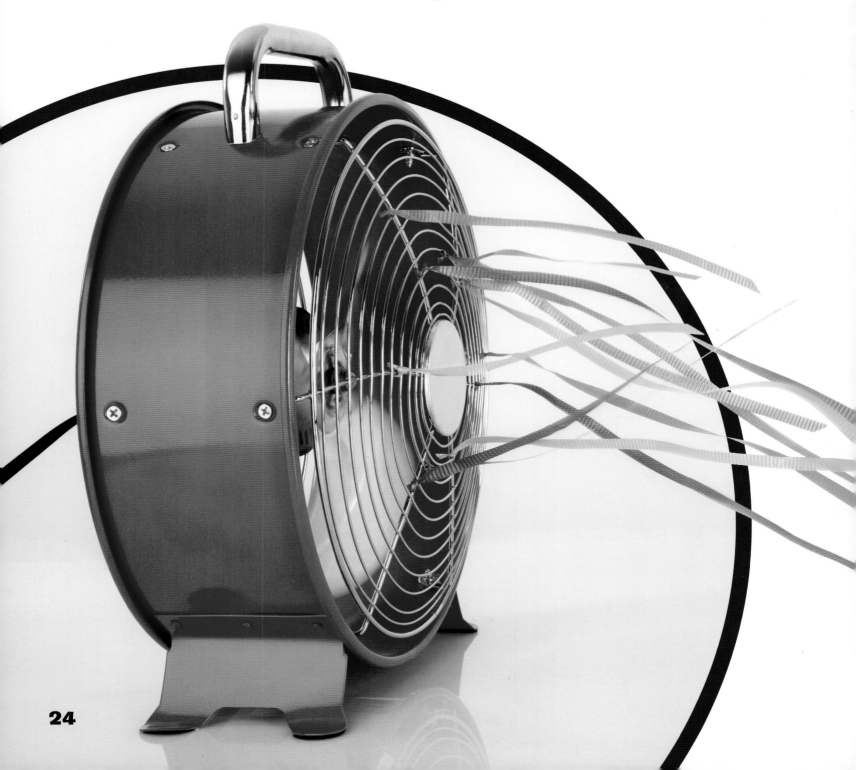

Magnets hold up pictures. They hold up signs. Credit cards use magnets to help people buy things.

The world would be very different
without magnets.

Magnets make our lives easier and safer.
They make our lives more fun too!

Move it with magnets!

Magnets move things made of steel. This activity will show you how magnetism works through plastic and water.

What you need:

2.5 x 2.5 centimetres (1 x 1 inch) square of thin green plastic
scissors

a stapler
a large plastic cup
water
a magnet

What you do:

- Cut out a turtle shape from the plastic. Use the stapler to put a staple in the middle of the plastic.
- Fill the plastic cup half full with water.
- Gently lay the turtle in the water so it floats.
- Hold the cup in one hand. Drag the magnet on the outside of the cup to move the turtle.
- Can you make your turtle move backwards and forwards? Try using the magnet to make your turtle spin. Drag the magnet down the side of the cup to make your turtle dive. Drag the magnet up the cup to make the turtle climb out of the water.
- What other ways can you move your turtle with a magnet? If your turtle does not move, use a stronger magnet or less water.

GLOSSARY

attract pull something towards something else

carve cut a piece of wood, stone or other hard material into a particular shape

compass tool that shows the direction of the North Pole

invisible something you cannot see

magnetic field area around a magnet that has the power to attract other metals, usually iron or steel

opposite facing or moving in the other direction

pilot person who flies a jet or plane

repel push something away

sailor person who works as a member of the crew on a ship or boat

scrapyard area used to collect, store and sometimes sell materials that have been thrown away

FIND OUT MORE

BOOKS

All About Magnetism (All About Science), Angela Royston (Heinemann Raintree, 2016)

Forces and Magnets (Fact Cat: Science), Izzi Howell (Wayland, 2017)

Forces and Magnets (Moving Up With Science), Peter Riley (Franklin Watts, 2016)

WEBSITES

www.bbc.co.uk/guides/zpvcrdm
Learn about magnetic poles on this BBC website.

www.dkfindout.com/uk/science/magnets
Have a look at this website to find out more about magnets.

COMPREHENSION QUESTIONS

1. Name two types of metal that magnets can move.
2. Sailors, aeroplane pilots and hikers all use compasses. What is a compass? Hint: Use the glossary for help!
3. Magnets are used for many things. They are in fans, refrigerators and TVs. How many of the things listed in this book can you find in your house?

INDEX